The Boston Trilogy

Rub Out
Kevin White
Bosston

Other Poetry by Ed Barrett

Or Current Resident
Sheepshead Bay
Breezy Point
Practical Lullabies for Joe/Watteau Sky
(Collaboration with Joe Torra)
Common Preludes
The Leaves Are Something This Year
Theory of Transportation

BOSSTON

ED BARRETT

2008 : Pressed Wafer : Boston

Acknowledgments:

My thanks to Derek Fenner and Ryan Gallagher of Bootstrap Press for permission to quote a brief passage from "Seen or encountered in Boston" from *A Book of Prophecies* by John Wieners, edited by Michael Carr (Bootstrap Press, 2007).

Contents

Green Monster
eleven

Dianne Wilkerson Is Not Louise Day Hicks
seventeen

Bullet Points
twenty nine

Dice-K
forty one

Finneranegan's Wake
forty nine

The Murder of Children in Boston
Will Make Police Commissioner Davis
Look Like Cardinal Law
fifty seven

All Souls'
sixty five

Ourselves Alone
seventy three

John Wieners at Filene's
eighty three

Mass Transit
eighty nine

For Caitie and Ciara

Two thoughts were so mixed up I could not tell
                                        W. B. Yeats

This pattern was set early in her public career—on New Year's Day in 1991, to be exact. The night before, as counsel for the local NAACP, Wilkerson had secured a historic agreement from then Mayor Ray Flynn that the city would abide by a federal race-blind admissions policy for public housing, for the first time opening up South Boston projects to blacks and providing a half-billion-dollar settlement for any families that had been wrongfully excluded. At about 4 the next morning, Wilkerson was awakened by a telephone call from a man who did not identify himself but, in an eerily calm voice, said he had just come from a meeting in South Boston where five men had agreed to terms on a contract on her life. It was for $28,000, the man said, adding that this was more than they'd gotten for the hit on Whitey McGrail, a South Boston bookie who had been, Wilkerson happened to know, gunned down, possibly over a gambling debt, five years before. The contract called for Wilkerson to be dead by 8 p.m. Thursday, January 3—three days away. Why? Wilkerson asked. "Because there are too many fucking niggers." And why was he telling her this? "Because I was cut out of the deal." Wilkerson called her friend Joe Carter, then deputy police superintendent (and now the MBTA's chief of transit police), and Carter dialed the police commissioner, Mickey Roache, who called Wilkerson and told her to stay away from her windows.

Boston·Magazine (March 2006)

Green Monster

This young crop knows it. Sometimes I think I could stay here forever. Then I remember what all the fuss is about. State labs have data to prove it. So I spend lunch breaks on the hill taking blood samples from the soil. It will be hard to confide in anyone anymore.

L.L. Bean catalogs drifting down out of a Maine sky promising renewed life on this earth in press-free slacks and all-day comfort in shoes with advanced walking-platform construction: the sky-blue mailman's uniform as he stuffs them in the mailbox, stacks of catalogs raked in a corner of the sofa, sliding off, red and orange and yellow pages as I walk across the room.

She rescues the investigation simply by showing up: cloudy bra-straps on bronzed shoulders, fragments we learn this from. No one collected such things anymore. Lists, sure, but people who made them came from far away, and we wanted a local in the back row with a fresh haircut straight from his best friend's wedding with the bride on his arm.

A field buries the ones it began. You'd think the sky would rub the field's broad back. Yes, that's exactly what you'd think. A field stammers and falls, a Gore-Tex sky bays out saltily over Boston harbor. And they enjoyed success and levity in the mock-up stage, a roar that came from behind the scoreboard, dense and pulpy, illegible as rebar.

Dianne Wilkerson Is Not Louise Day Hicks

In the Mediatheque Room of the new Institute of Contemporary Art reinforced glass walls gave on to Boston harbor like the wheelhouse of an LNG tanker on its way to off-load in Everett. All the algorithms nothing could bring or anodyne or ghost in the phosphor night of the ICA.

Arrangements have not been disclosed, but Fan Pier was a big project: not just a new Southie, a new Boston, shiny as good teeth on a Cape Cod summer afternoon, a John Hynes Boston, his even, year-round golf tan smiling over a deal at the Institute of Contemporary Anthony's Pier 4.

Only MBTA Transit Police could be trusted. Maybe a few Chinese detectives working family abuse on the Boston PD. Even they were trained by Irish sergeants and listened to Celtic Twilight on 91.9 Saturday afternoons.

A Roxbury Annunciation was a stray bullet through a second-floor apartment window severing a child's spine. A Dorchester *Pietà* found a mother, outside belief and disbelief, outside words and language, draping her child over the metal lap of a wheelchair donated by Dunkin' Donuts to take the Orange Line to Downtown Crossing.

Police Commissioner Kathleen O'Toole and Whitey Butler Yeats were no flight into Egypt with a Cape Verdean child at An Garda Síochána na hÉireann headquarters in Phoenix Park, Dublin. They, each alone, vanished into Boston's radioactive dream of Irish transcendence. He wouldn't even put on Rubbermaid kitchen gloves to yank out "Bucky" Barrett's teeth after he shot him in the head because no one in South Boston ever caught AIDS.

Who could be who in Boston: more reminder than question toward the end of his shift as a transit cop and the start of an argument fluent as song: William Bratton rode the MBTA Transit Police all the way to New York Police Commissioner where he let Giuliani run the NYPD like the Royal Ulster Constabulary—white over black, Long Island over Harlem, same as Protestant over Belfast Catholic. Rudy played it like Shankill while Bratton transitioned the force from RUC to PSNI, Public Service of Northern Ireland. *Public Service!* And he looked around to make sure he hadn't said it out loud on the Red line to JFK/UMass in Dorchester. Bratton used CompStat to prick out precinct captains who didn't measure up. Imagine, as his argument modulated with a kind of grudging wonder, reaching into Staten Island or Queens through a computer screen at One Police Plaza. Pure Public Service. The old RUC badge, its royal crown now alongside a harp, a shamrock and the saltire of Saint fucking Patrick.

The new IRA was just drugs and Polish whores, ordinary organized crime hiding money from the Criminal Assets Bureau. Sinn Féin disarms, becomes the fastest growing political party, wants seats in the government North and South. How could Whitey Butler Yeats run guns to Belfast on the *Valhalla* out of Boston and not have known the informer *on board* who gives it up to the British and make money from both sides? Charlie Haughey's dead and buried in his French shirts. Developers in the Gaeltacht pay cash and race like Vikings in ribbed inflatables with twin 200 hp Honda outboard engines. After 9/11 FBI and British MI5 share intelligence, honor their deals and informants, themselves alone in a delirious desert. Whitey Yeats ghosts his way around a transcendent west of witness protection. Yeats likes big cars. Northern Ireland has good roads.

With the flick of a finger hooked out of a spreadsheet Bratton turned sainted relics into dust. I don't want to thaw out Ted Williams' head for fuck sake. A computer class at Suffolk nights, I could ride the T all the way to State Police headquarters on Day Boulevard.

On acres of aboveground parking lots, the anti-Big Dig of Fan Pier stammered into night. They'd never forgive Wilkerson denied South Boston delegates their party credentials at the Springfield convention when Dukakis ran for President. *All fate is personal,* says the phosphor night in Greek outside the ICA.

All the algorithms nothing could bring or anodyne or ghost, "what matter who it be," in the Mediatheque Room of the Institute of Contemporary Anthony's Pier 4, in night class at Suffolk University.

Bullet Points

Boston is not Boston. Static like that it meant nothing. Words were not words, there was only presentation. There is no language, only communication. There is no thought, only information. There is value accrued already owed on a different project.

BOSTON

IS

NOT

appears after an idealized Boston skyline seen from the leafy, sterile lap of Killian Court across the Charles at MIT opened on a large-screen projection from his MacBook Pro. Siena Beacon Hill, uglier financial district buildings Photoshopped out and **BOSTON** draped over the gold State Capitol dome; the old John Hancock building's tower flashing **IS**; and the CITGO sign (cropped closer in this PowerPoint slide) with **NOT** in neon. Then, slithering up the side of the Hancock Tower's flat-screen TV face, one animated letter crawling after the other like sci-fi creatures escaped from a biotech lab at MIT,

B
O
S
T
O
N

Silent pressure of thumb against remote, a dot, a ball of light out of night-sky nothingness, its trajectory an outfielder's certainty that he hadn't lost it in the lights as he punches his glove anticipating the final out of the inning.

- A roar that came from behind the scoreboard

- Boston was not Boston

- Asterisk of nothing through the back of her head

- Words are not words

- To plead a special case, some exception

Radiant, rocketing toward the skyline, an indistinct symbol diving at static buildings. Screen wipe, and the Green Monster, its hand-operated squares for innings, three by three by four, up to the tenth, then R H E and P, filling with the letters

BOS   TON   ISBO STON

™ crashing into the final **N** as fireworks explode above Fenway Park.

Dice-K

"Let me steal," as he started his wrap-up, "from a famous writer who was also a statesman of his native fields—a developer, if you will, who built a theater out of the rubble of his native Dublin and gave his countrymen, and the world, a championship team with new ideas...."

If they could simulate their idea of Boston's elusive, fugitive soul on these fields of undeveloped parking lots in South Boston, they could export it across oceans to places that existed only as design plans, Songdo City in South Korea, or Dubai with its indoor ski resort built over a delirious eternal desert.

"Boston is a brand," he said firmly with a directness he knew would not insult his audience but showed respect for the unwritten codes and allegiances they had made their money from: a few of them after a brief time in the business; others at the summit of a longer career who knew how expensive memory and sentiment were and could afford these waters of human existence.

Inside the Boston Convention and Exhibition Center (*Built by users, for users,* says its homepage), its image from Google Earth a capsized hull along the I-90 Connector in South Boston, his miked voice, through an acoustical design miscalculation, swallowed up in dead corners of the reconfigurable meeting room. If you were seated in one of these hollows, brushing your suited knees against thick, unyielding linen draped over a round breakfast table, the clatter of cutlery against convention-grade plate, you heard only splashes of his peroration about images of Boston: Jack Nicholson (laughter throughout the room); *The Departed* (laughter and applause); Matt Damon (louder, more respectful applause); a sound like the word "terror" at which you leaned forward and heard a sound like the word "beauty."

"The city's changing, ladies and gentleman. We've changed. And if I may steal from a poet you probably don't remember from high school English class—although" (slight cock of his head to a priest on the dais) "don't confess it—A terrific beauty is born!"

A young arm throwing for the media, a real gun, his face a mask of professional disinterest—a cop's face, Mary's Annunciation face—he took the dirt of the crown of the field, rubbed it between the tips of his fingers, and what did not crumble he threw back down. The Red Sox organization had already made back its signing money off Japanese media deals. He fulfilled his contract, pulled the trigger in one symbolic act, and now would be hunted by fugitive Boston dreams.

Finneranegan's Wake

Boston is a small town, a two-horse town. Schools and biotech, or schools and media. Not cosmopolitan, not a world stage: a staging area, a seminary or seminal fluid like the ocean it came from and was built over. The ocean it shifts effluent through. The ocean which flows over it as cool sea breezes in August or under it as groundwater chewing through its birthday-cake foundations. The ocean Boston emulates in its bit-stream flood of financial services, university research and sports.

Its dead simply will not stay buried.

And what was wrong with building into that ocean where *We perish'd, each alone* could be inscribed on walls and ceiling panels of the I-90 Connector tunnel? To reclaim parts of language and death that belonged to each of us, ourselves alone in the smoke of neighborhoods, garbled sentences of dirt and light stammered out of Boston, dense and pulpy, illegible as rebar?

The soul in its witness protection program, invisible as the period at the end of this sentence.

A grammar you knew by heart, a sequence of endings in place of the wash of tides in Boston harbor, uncarried of words to drift, mind to mind, as thought or image, as expectation or desire, repeated, accented as if for the first time.

The soul is a Boston of spoken words, accented as if for the first time along the linings of the heart of the Big Dig tunnels, WRKO morning drive talk with Tom Finneran on the commute in-town listening to his analysis of your life as it is lived within and without the city limits and the protection of CCTV monitoring the roads, a cellphone for your kids to check in with or if your engine overheats on I-93. His analysis filtered through gills on the side of his neck which he grew when he served on the Massachusetts Biotechnology Council before he washed overboard and lost his pirate's pension to raise his family in Mattapan, and education—its price tag is insane! Can Matsuzaka handle Boston media raking him over the coals of every summer barbecue with the game on? All the beauty of Boston terrors one tunes in to so not to have to say, *But I beneath a rougher sea / And whelm'd in deeper gulphs than he.*

The Murder of Children in Boston Will Make Police Commissioner Davis Look Like Cardinal Law

these
are words, always there when
the big cries wear themselves out.

William Corbett

Whitey Butler Yeats knew how to shrink to the size of the period at the end of this sentence. This young crop fields GPS coordinates across Google Earth on post-age-stamp cellphone screens with the certainty of an outfielder under the final out of the inning.

Words not words

T L8 c u   5mn   luv u

Letters and numbers alight to the touch of a child's
fingers at the Jackson Square MBTA Station.

Phosphors of faith and insufficiency, windows lit up in the early dark, eyeless in necessity and contempt of acts of matchless wonder and emptiness.

Texting a night sky marbled with zodiacs and satellites triangulating his last location to the point at the end of a sentence.

Arrangements have not been disclosed.

In lieu of flowers, the body to uncarry itself as necessary and sufficient, ourselves alone, with hardly any subjects to interrogate anything for very long, not for all the tea in Boston harbor.

in memory, Luis Gerena, Jason Fernandes, Emmanuel B. Saintil

All Souls'

Boston's dead simply will not stay buried.

Ralph Waldo "The Rifleman" Emerson and Deborah Hussey Thoreau, their Platonic dream of winter sunlight reflected off the sunflower dome of the Commonwealth of Massachusetts State Capitol Building, its pilings driven into Back Bay's Flemish mound "like birthday candles into a moist cake."

A loud flailing in answer to dreams of permanence,
the Big Dig uncarried by a road underground where
it belongs to souls of the departed, a road in Greek,
and the Institute of Contemporary Anthony's Pier 4.

A road underground with all the dutchments of the body, foretold or ordained or probable, its carbon-fiber laws of length and duration, its human diffuse ichor.

Deborah Hussey Thoreau had several more lives to live and could not spare any more time for one where the damned howled away their hearts in a useless transcendent mound off I-93.

Whitey Butler Yeats held it tight, a thought that, in it wound, he could run like Boris Karloff in *The Mummy*, run in the world's despite: "The mind is weak, and I can shrink to the size of a period at the end of this sentence, and in it need no other thing." He was a ghost-lover all right, and grew more arrogant being a ghost.

Ourselves Alone

Ramp L off the I-90 Connector is marked Exit 20, and ultimately, truth is, there is no bedrock layer under Boston to interrogate as one interrogates, for example, an ocean, or more correctly, the ocean's lace panties around your ankles on M Street Beach. Aw, c'mon, what do you want to know anyway, Mr. HartCrane@OceanDivers.com? Or, more correctly, *how* do you want to know "being both chance and choice?" As Genzyme knows? As the Massachusetts Biotechnology Council or the Whitehead Institute at MIT: stranded, sequenced residue?

—Two more again, please.

Stoli and grapefruit juice. Just what we didn't know we wanted until we tasted it, different from our usual, each alone, but perfect just when you don't expect it because you don't expect anything to be perfect and, let's face it, perfection comes and goes on its own, the harbor vessel one watches from the deck of the ICA. And is there anything more reassuring than the complex and complete workings of a boat in winter belling out against the season, its rime-crusted gunwales and wheelhouse stars?

Added pleasure, talk not too different from the usual pissing and moaning, followed by gossip, followed by joking about what we pissed and moaned at, looking and joking about who is walking to the restrooms near our table in the fullness of the usual bar, the usual conversation which is music in friendship, variations and improvisations on themes, waiting and not waiting for the new note and a time we tune the rigging for weather.

Drink Asahi "Super Dry" beer! Dice-K in Red Sox jersey before a blue-screen backdrop of cheering fans at Fenway. "Simple faith/Licensed to take the meanings that we love," creaks the deck of a trawler in Japanese, its rime-ice glitter and wheelhouse stars warm and trashy off Dorchester Bay.

How the landscape changes, all of a sudden inching up on eternity, the soul it unravels, snagged on body and blood. Harvard stadium's new bubble dome, spaceship silver, alien in Allston: February spring training, young arms warming up, the popcorn *pop pop pop* of baseballs exploding into catchers' mitts; metallic sing of aluminum bats, ceiling bolts snapping in the I-90 Connector tunnel.

Meditations upon unknown thought, inevitable and just, sequencing ornamental scrolls to waves churning across the loss of eternity. Who is not Louise Day Hicks to *Restore Our Alienated Rights*, a roar that comes from beneath the scoreboard, dense and pulpy, illegible as rebar?

The soul in its witness protection program, radioactive dreams of Irish transcendence and communion, body and blood to deny South Boston delegates party credentials at the Democratic convention in Springfield, Massachusetts. There is no language, spaceship algorithms nothing could bring or anodyne ghost to run in the world's despite.

John Wieners at Filene's

"Seen or encountered in Boston," wrote John Wieners in his notebook. Real or desired, a vision: Barbara Stanwyck, who had wardrobe show her stomach but asked them to cover the rest of her body, which she said was flawed. Can you hear her saying "flawed" in a Brooklyn accent? Description wants to cup your face in its hands, cradle a telephone in the crook of its transparent arm, whispering, "It's impossible to know," and "We all stand revealed." Barbara Stanwyck had wardrobe describe her body according to her body's logic: "Give a girl a break, will ya? Yeah, like that. Aw, you're a peach!" And description wants to know the impossible too, set it down for the record, a silver ribbon studded with rhinestones. If you're lucky, you hear someone mean it in terms of a clarity of feeling: "I'd do anything for you"—not totally "out there" or anything too deported from the laity of believers and the truths they take by the hand where a diamond cutout over the midriff shows Barbara Stanwyck's stomach. "Why now?", it goes in the dark, "Why, when everything was just beginning to change, my life on track again?" To cradle her body with clarity and deportment is all she was asking in her crooked accent, embracing wardrobe like a doll, a living doll.

85

"Like birthday candles into a moist cake." Boston's Back Bay, built on wooden pilings driven into landfill, is sinking. A consulting engineer from Ireland, he was interested in final effect chemistry. "Nobody gives a shit about the origin of molecules!," he said in a rough Dublin accent. He said this so forcefully that for a moment I believed ordinary people spent time thinking about molecules, and that when they thought about them they also thought "I don't give a shit about their origins!" Dublin in Irish is *Baile Átha Cliath*, Town of the Ford of the Reed Hurdles, although most of those t's and h's you don't pronounce, and the l's are liquidy and the whole thing is kind of gargley mouthwashed in the back of the throat. Irish is vanishing from the stony fields of Ireland, heather like fresh Brillo pads purpling hillsides, scraping clay off your boots and the skin off your legs if you make the mistake of trying to walk through it.

Everything is the case: I must have asked about a certain flower I saw in West Kerry so he brought a guide book to flowers which he opened to a picture of a beautiful but not especially exotic eye-blue flower identified first in Latin and then by its English name, which was "Yesterday, Today and Tomorrow." I thought, "That's an odd flower name," although perfectly expressive of the staying power of Latin suavely enveloping every dangling piece of fruit and vegetation the branch of days can promote. I didn't say anything, and since he didn't mention it either we just "processed this bit of information" as we say now about placing things in, but really out of, memory.

"Seen or encountered in Boston," wrote John Wieners, remembered or imagined or desired: "Gloria Swanson at Filene's cut shortly after Michele Morgan arrived avec D.D. Babs Stanwyck bypassed in shocking silk." Filene's closed for redevelopment by the Hynes group, Wieners' body unclaimed for days, IDed through a CVS receipt found in his pocket by a nurse who wouldn't let her case go cold. "Dyes were everything," said the engineer from Dublin over more pints, and he explained how modern chemistry took its start from commercial dyeing processes. "These stripes," he was saying as he pinched the sleeve of my shirt, "My God, now they could have vats of colors instead of using ..." and he paused, looking for what colors in shirts were once made from: "Berries?" I offered. "Berries!" he shouted, "Now you could have a feckin' stripe on every feckin' shirt." People were happy because of this, he was implying, and I had to agree with his unstated conclusion because I was happy with my shirt, and I don't give a shit about origins or their vegetable endings, and sometimes my happiness is like big vats of yesterday, today and tomorrow chemical blue.

Mass Transit

Necessity gave the cold, cold hand a glove

Moondoggie, in *Gidget*

A few. Now five. Now all these kids skating on the Charles River, our first hard freeze, some with hockey sticks sweeping an invisible puck. The reason the Dutch were so happy and prosperous was the frozen canals they skated on is a thought they are not aware of having; it is a thought the Charles River is having about them, including them in Wheelwright's dream of bridges from the Netherlands, each a windmill blade turning to a world above water with a question unfulfilled.

The body pleading its case for insufficiency: balance unattainable except by those for whom loyalty is impossible; how it offers to reach into the cone-shaped silence of a river like a child reaching for a shiny stone.

We are tempted here on earth by symmetry and example to reach beyond bounds in our wooden shoes. On their shoulders prophecy and measure, like two big buckets of milk, sweep skaters away to the end of something fidgeting with its bra strap. They decline as grammar declines an immediate language of expectation and memory, how the outcome only used necessity as we float backwards through the truth.

Wheelwright's ode in Dutch to the American Civil War: *To A Father By A Son,* unironic as the No. 66 bus over the Larz Anderson bridge to Brookline and Michael Dukakis who must've thought he could do material for Whitey "The Mummy" Yeats and the South Boston Rat Pack at the St. Patrick's Day breakfast, his face the grave of the joke he was about to tell, a regular Joey Bishop.